Canada Day

By Patricia J. Murphy

Consultants
Nanci Vargus, Ed.D.
Primary Multiage Teacher
Decatur Township Schools, Indianapolis, Indiana

Katharine A. Kane, Reading Specialist
Former Language Arts Coordinator
San Diego County Office of Education

Children's Press®
A Division of Scholastic Inc.
New York   Toronto   London   Auckland   Sydney
Mexico City   New Delhi   Hong Kong
Danbury, Connecticut

Designer: Herman Adler Design
Photo Researcher: Caroline Anderson
The photo on the cover shows a Canada Day parade.

Library of Congress Cataloging-in-Publication Data

Murphy, Patricia J., 1963-
  Canada Day / by Patricia J. Murphy.
      p. cm. — (Rookie read-about holidays)
Includes index.
Summary: Explains the history, importance, and celebration of Canada
Day.
  ISBN 0-516-22662-2 (lib. bdg.)   0-516-27487-2 (pbk.)
  1. Canada Day—Juvenile literature. [1. Canada Day. 2. Holidays.]
I. Title. II. Series.
  F1033 .M976 2002
  394.263—dc21

                                    2002005487

CHILDREN'S PRESS, AND ROOKIE READ-ABOUT®,
and associated logos are trademarks and or registered trademarks
of Grolier Publishing Co., Inc. SCHOLASTIC and associated logos
are trademarks and or registered trademarks of Scholastic Inc.

1 2 3 4 5 6 7 8 9 10 R 11 10 09 08 07 06 05 04 03 02

Do you celebrate Canada Day?

Canada Day is a special holiday. It is Canada's birthday.

Canada is a country in North America.

Canada Day is Canada's biggest holiday. It is held on July 1 each year. When the date falls on a Sunday, people celebrate it on Monday.

July 2003

Sunday	Monday	Tuesday	Wednesday	Thursday	Friday	Saturday
		1	2	3	4	5
6	7	8	9	10	11	12
13	14	15	16	17	18	19
20	21	22	23	24	25	26
27	28	29	30	31		

Long ago, the provinces of
Canada were called colonies.
They were ruled by the
country of Great Britain.
Several of them wanted
to join together to become
their own country.

On July 1, 1867, Great Britain passed the British North America Act. This act made a new country called the Dominion of Canada.

It let the colonies set up their own government.

The British North America
Act also listed rules for the
new country to follow.

The Dominion of Canada
was still part of Great Britain.

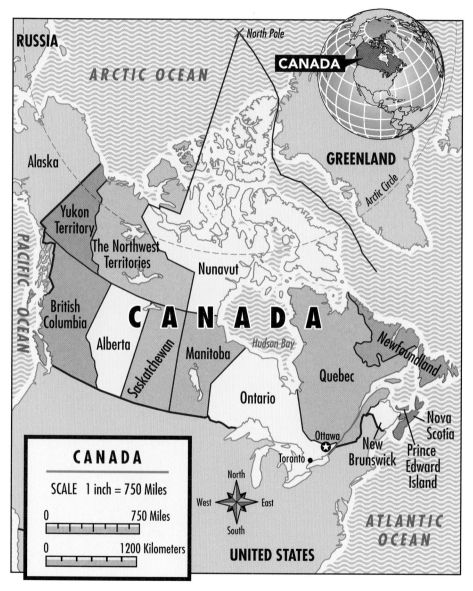

RUSSIA

ARCTIC OCEAN

North Pole

CANADA

GREENLAND

Arctic Circle

Alaska

Yukon
Territory

The Northwest
Territories

Nunavut

PACIFIC OCEAN

British
Columbia

Alberta

Saskatchewan

Manitoba

Hudson Bay

Newfoundland

C A N A D A

Quebec

Ontario

Nova
Scotia

Ottawa

Toronto

New
Brunswick

Prince
Edward
Island

ATLANTIC
OCEAN

UNITED STATES

CANADA

SCALE   1 inch = 750 Miles

0   750 Miles

0   1200 Kilometers

North

West   East

South

14

In 1879, Canada decided to call July 1 Dominion Day.

Over the years, more provinces joined Canada. Today, Canada has ten provinces and three territories.

In 1982, Canada became an independent country. That means Canada was no longer part of Great Britain. The holiday's name was changed to Canada Day.

18

On Canada Day, people who live in Canada celebrate Canada's independence. People celebrate in many different ways.

Some people wear red and white. These are the colors in Canada's flag.

Some people paint maple
leaves on their faces.
The maple leaf is a symbol
of Canada.

There are parades on Canada Day. People watch Canadian Mounties ride in the parades on their horses.

People set off fireworks
at night.

On Canada Day, Canadians
may also sing "O Canada!"
It is Canada's anthem,
or song.

The song is about how
Canadians are proud of
their country and of
being Canadian.

That is what Canada Day
is all about!

Words You Know

birthday

Canada's flag

Canadian Mounties

celebrate

fireworks

maple leaf

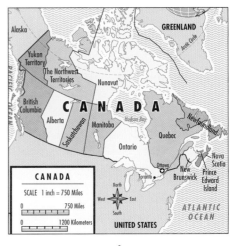

provinces

31

Index

About the Author

Patricia J. Murphy writes children's storybooks, non-fiction books, early readers, and poetry. She also writes for magazines, corporations, and museums. She lives in Northbrook, IL. She wants to thank her Canadian friends, Clyde, Elise, Gwen, Doris, the Canadian Consulate, and the Canadian Embassy for their help with this book.

Photo Credits

Photographs © 2002: AP/Wide World Photos/Fred Chartrand: 17; Corbis Images/Gunter Marx: cover; H. Armstrong Roberts, Inc./H. Sutton: 13; Masterfile/Rommel: 3, 30 bottom left; North Wind Picture Archives: 10; Spectrum Stock: 21, 25, 31 bottom left, 31 top right (Denis Drever/NCC), 26 (Duofoto), 22, 29, 30 bottom right (Tony Mihok), 4, 18, 30 top, 31 top left (Frank Scott); The Image Works/Topham Picturepoint: 9.

Map p. 14, 31 bottom right by Bob Italiano